Lifting the Burden

An Introduction to Spiritual Principles That Will Transform
Your Life

by Brian Oxley

*To Sharon,*

*With all good wishes,*

*Brian Oxley*

GW00492739

## My Journey

From the age of 13, until the age of 57, my main focus in life had been politics.

However, up until the age of 13, I had hardly bothered to even read a newspaper. However, one day, it was as though a switch had been flicked and I found myself getting more and more drawn into the subject and reading as much as I could.

The key issue that seemed to capture my imagination was the thought of helping others to lift their burdens. Indeed this theme followed me as I matured as a political person.

I worked hard to get into Politics. I followed the traditional educational path of going to University before eventually getting the opportunity to work professionally for Members of the British House of Commons, for nearly 30 years, and as a Local Authority Councillor in Brighton and Hove, for over 16 years.

However, in 1992, something happened that would literally change my life.

I was told by two Mediums, independently of each other, and about six months apart, that I needed to attend a Spiritualist Church. To be honest I didn't know they even existed!

I found one near where my partner (now my husband) and I were living at the time and I started to attend.

Some 12 years later I began to sit in an awareness class and to develop my own Spiritual awareness.

# Introduction

Working with Spirit is a profoundly simple concept that encompasses key elements such as embracing Love and Trust, facing Fear, and recognising the Power of the Law of Cause and Effect, also referred to as Universal Law. When we act from a place of Love, our actions are grounded in truth and integrity. We selflessly act without expecting personal gain, deriving our motivation from a deep sense of joy and understanding.

On the other hand, when Fear drives our actions, we often hinder our own progress, resulting in a challenging life where our aspirations and efforts fail to materialise as we had hoped. Fear has a detrimental effect on human beings, diminishing their potential, while Love has the opposite effect, uniting and elevating individuals.

Working with Spirit not only brings us comfort but also provides us with guidance and companionship. It reveals the eternal truth that we are all interconnected, forming a unified whole through the power of Universal Love.

In life, people constantly seek security and certainty. They desire to move forward in ways that align with their personal interests and bring them satisfaction. Fear, however, frequently drives individuals as they worry about scarcity. They witness famines, wars, and deprivations in various forms each day. Yet, it is essential to recognise that the Universe holds unlimited resources for everyone. The activation of these resources relies on our intentional creation of life through Love and Trust instead of Fear and Doubt. By living in this way, no one needs to go without.

You have a birthright to manifest on Earth the unique gifts and skills you were born with. By doing so, you serve your fellow human beings while also receiving the income, acknowledgement, and respect of others with whom you interact. Each person's birthright differs; for some, it may be to become great artists, while for others, it could be running successful businesses or providing care for a loved one in need. The crucial aspect lies in discovering what is right for you and determining how you can achieve it. This process leads to many lessons - the key reason for our decision to live on Earth for a span of years.

In summary, the core essence of working with Spirit revolves around Love, Fear, and the Law of Cause and Effect. Acting from Love brings unity and elevates us, while Fear hinders our progress and diminishes our potential. By tapping into the power of Universal Love, we can find comfort, guidance, and the realisation of our connectedness. It is important to understand that in the abundant Universe, resources are plentiful when approached with Love and Trust. Embracing our unique gifts and serving others allows us to receive the rewards and recognition we deserve. Ultimately, the path to fulfilment lies in discovering our own purpose and taking the necessary steps to achieve it.

Questions to ponder

1.   What do you REALLY want to get out of life?

2.   Where have you tried and failed before?

3.   What would have to happen in order for you to believe in your dreams again?

# Universal Law

The Universal Law governs the intricate relationship between our thoughts, actions, and words, and the responses we receive from the world around us. It illuminates the principle that our intentions, whether positive or negative, create ripples that eventually return to us, very often amplified in magnitude. By embracing this law, we can gain profound insight into the dynamics of the spiritual realm and harness its transformative potential for personal growth and fulfilment.

At its core, the Universal Law asserts that kindness, love, forgiveness, and generosity are not only noble virtues but also powerful tools that shape our reality. When we radiate positivity and benevolence towards others, the Universe responds by mirroring these qualities back into our lives. Consequently, the more we cultivate compassion and goodwill, the more we attract the same positive energy from the world, forming a virtuous cycle of reciprocity.

Conversely, negative thoughts and actions carry their own weight and effect. Engaging in gossip, harbouring feelings of dislike, and being critical of others can lead to an undesirable feedback loop. The Universal Law ensures that these unkind vibrations echo back to us, potentially perpetuating a cycle of disharmony and dissatisfaction.

To avoid this, it becomes imperative to monitor our thoughts and intentions, striving to align them with the higher principles of love and understanding. If we are often negative, we simply have to catch ourselves and flip the thought. If I am negative and thinking this, what can I think to be positive? What is the contrast to my negative thought?

While the Universal Law operates consistently, its results may not always be immediately evident in the physical realm. A smile offered to someone might not trigger an immediate response, and an unkind remark may not appear to affect our lives in the short term. Yet, it is crucial to recognise that the effects of our intentions resonate in the unseen plane of existence, working towards a manifestation that aligns with the energy we emit. Thus, patience and faith become essential virtues in navigating this Universal process.

A profound example of the Universal Law's operation lies in the realm of abundance and prosperity. Someone may have amassed considerable wealth, yet if their underlying beliefs convey a sense of scarcity and fear of loss, they will perpetually remain impoverished, unable to experience the true benefits of their wealth. Our thoughts and intentions have the power to either unlock the abundance that surrounds us or confine us within the walls of our self-imposed limitations.

The transformative potential of the Universal Law was vividly illustrated in a personal experience. Facing the challenge of moving from an apartment that didn't suit our needs, my husband and I sought to harness the power of intention and manifest a favourable outcome. Through determination and an unwavering focus on finding a solution, we aligned our thoughts and actions with our desired goal. As a result, a plan materialised that led us back to our previous home, ushering in a positive change in life.

To leverage the Universal Law effectively, it is essential to cultivate mindfulness and awareness of our thoughts, emotions, and intentions. By consciously choosing to radiate positivity, love, and compassion, we not only enrich our lives but also contribute to a harmonious collective consciousness. Simultaneously, we should remain vigilant against negative thought patterns, striving to replace them with constructive and uplifting ones.

In conclusion, the Universal Law represents a profound spiritual principle governing our existence. It reminds us that the energy we emit through our thoughts, actions, and words creates a feedback loop that shapes our reality. By embracing the power of positive intentions and cultivating kindness, we can harness this law to transform our lives and contribute to a more compassionate and harmonious world. As we internalise this wisdom, may we all embark on a journey of self-discovery and growth, guided by the timeless and unwavering principles of the Universal Law.

Questions to ponder

1.   What stops you TRUSTING?

2.   How do you decide how to set your goals in your life?

3.   Is your work really fulfilling you and is this what you want to do for the rest of your life?

Forgiveness

Many people misunderstand forgiveness.

Forgiveness does not mean saying to someone that what they have done to you in malice or said about you negatively is OK.

Forgiveness in Spiritual terms is about learning the lesson from the experience you have had and then moving forward knowing you have taken the power from the problems.

You can forgive and forget, so long as you learn the lesson and ensure you do not place yourself in the same position to have to learn the lesson again.

The truth is that living by Spiritual principles takes action, thought and discipline on our part. It is also important to remember that there are no exceptions to the rules. What you give out will always come back.

If a person lives from a position of hatred and unforgiving they will not be able to move on from their ordeal because they will lock in the energy of the problem. They will not live a full life until they remove the sense of being wronged.

The truth we have to learn is that there is a lesson in everything. To fulfil our role we have to look for this. This is not easy but it can be done.

There are many examples of where someone has wronged another and the  person has decided not to live in anger but reach out to embrace the wrongdoer. In 1981, for example, after he was shot, President Reagan prayed with Cardinal Cooke for the man who had tried to kill him. Pope John Paul actually prayed with his attacker, after an assassination attempt.

Forgiveness is a foundational spiritual principle that transcends mere interpersonal dynamics. It's a transformative journey, one that reshapes our inner landscape and alters our perception of the world. Let's delve deeper into the spiritual dimensions of forgiveness, exploring its nuances and implications for personal growth and harmony.

To understand forgiveness in a spiritual context, it's crucial to recognise that it's not about condoning harmful actions or dismissing personal pain. Instead, it's about releasing the burden of resentment and anger that shackles us to past experiences. When we forgive, we're not declaring that a wrong act was acceptable; rather, we're choosing to liberate ourselves from the continuous impact of that act on our lives.

Spiritual forgiveness involves a deep inner transformation. It's a conscious decision to let go of grudges and bitterness, regardless of whether the other person deserves it or even seeks it. This doesn't imply forgetfulness; rather, it's about remembering without the sting of pain. The essence of forgiveness is not in erasing memories but in changing our reaction to them.

At the heart of this process is the understanding that each experience, especially the painful ones, holds a valuable lesson. These lessons are the spiritual gold, mined from the ore of our struggles. By embracing these lessons, we empower ourselves. We shift from being victims of our past to architects of our future.

Forgiveness, however, is not a one-time event but a continuous process. It's a practice that requires patience, compassion, and repeated effort. Each act of forgiveness is a step towards spiritual maturity, an ascent on the ladder of personal growth.

This principle also emphasizes the law of reciprocity in spiritual terms. What we emit into the universe — be it love, hatred, forgiveness, or resentment — tends to return to us in various forms. A heart embittered by unforgiveness not only poisons its own well-being but also repels the joy and peace that life offers.

Moreover, forgiveness is not just a personal endeavour; it has a collective dimension. When we forgive, we contribute to the healing of the world. We break cycles of pain and retaliation, paving the way for reconciliation and peace. As individuals, our acts of forgiveness ripple outwards, influencing our communities and, ultimately, the broader fabric of society.

Historically, there have been numerous instances where individuals, despite experiencing profound wrongs, chose the path of forgiveness. These acts often seem counterintuitive, yet they exemplify the transformative power of forgiveness. From world leaders to everyday individuals, those who embrace forgiveness often find a deeper sense of purpose and peace.

In conclusion, forgiveness is a profound spiritual principle that offers freedom, healing, and growth. It's a path that requires courage, humility, and resilience. By embracing forgiveness, we not only heal ourselves but also contribute to the healing of the world around us. It is, indeed, a principle that illuminates the path towards a more compassionate and harmonious existence.

Questions to ponder

1.    How can you live from a position of forgiveness at all times?

2.    How do you know when you have truly released the power someone has over you by forgiving them? (Hint: it is not about just saying the words!)

3.    How do you look for the opportunities from situations that you perceived as 'bad' or 'difficult'?

Trust

Trust, a cornerstone of our spiritual journey, is far from blind hope; it is a proactive and dynamic force that involves working diligently to bring about positive outcomes in our lives. To trust in the Spirit means embracing the belief that our efforts, combined with the Universal Power, work in harmonious synergy to manifest results that are ultimately for our highest benefit. Key to this principle is having faith in the unseen, acknowledging that though the power may be imperceptible, it is an integral part of the greatest force in the Universe.

In our lives, we may encounter instances where our desires remain unfulfilled, and unexpected outcomes unfold. In the heat of such moments, it is all too easy to hastily pass judgments and condemn the events that transpire. However, a longer view reveals that what initially appears as disappointment may, in fact, be our most significant turning points. Trusting that everything happens for a reason liberates us from self-recrimination when things go awry, enabling us to look ahead with anticipation, knowing that new opportunities lie ahead.

Drawing from personal experience, I once pursued the ambition of becoming a Member of Parliament, pouring my heart and effort into the endeavour. While my attempts in this direction proved unsuccessful, life had different plans for me. It led me to an unexpected path where I eventually became the Leader of a Local Authority, entrusted with being the political leader of a city of 250,000 people, and overseeing a substantial budget of £750m. This twist of fate showed me that sometimes, not getting what we initially wanted opens doors to other opportunities.

Another momentous instance occurred when I made the decision to delve into full-time politics in 1987. However, financial constraints loomed as the money available for researchers in the House of Commons was limited. To make ends meet, I needed to offer research services to two Members of Parliament, securing their agreement before the General Election. Though I had obtained in-principle commitments from two potential MPs before the election, post-election circumstances took an unexpected turn. One MP reaffirmed their intent to employ me, but the other unexpectedly opted against needing my services.

At this crossroads, uncertainty weighed heavily, but I refused to succumb to doubt. Determined to find my way forward, I decided to leave my current job and simultaneously reached out to numerous MPs in hopes of securing that elusive second opportunity. As the days ticked by, nearing the end of my safe public sector job, I had to trust that the right chance would appear. Just in time, a request for an interview with an MP seeking someone with experience in the very field I specialised in came my way. Although the prospect felt risky, an instinct to trust urged me forward. To my delight, it paid off immensely! I found my second MP and embarked on my career working as a Researcher in Parliament.

The essence of trusting in the Spirit lies not in passivity, but in proactive dedication and unwavering belief in the unseen forces that shape our reality. It is a journey of co-creation, where we collaborate with the Universal Power to steer our lives toward their highest purpose. Amid uncertainties and disappointments, having faith in divine order allows us to navigate life's twists and turns with resilience and grace.

In conclusion, trust is a potent force that propels us forward in our spiritual evolution. Far from mere hope, it is a dynamic engagement with the Universe, where our efforts merge with unseen energies to manifest the best possible outcomes. Learning to trust amidst life's uncertainties frees us from self-criticism and enables us to embrace the unfolding of our paths with anticipation. My personal experiences are a testament to the transformative power of trust, revealing that life's detours often lead to grander destinations. As we continue to embrace trust and faith, may we uncover the profound wisdom that lies within life's intricacies, and find solace in knowing that the Universe works in mysterious yet benevolent ways.

Questions to ponder

1.    How do you know you are moving in the right direction when you seem to be making no progress?

2.    When has someone let you down and you later realised they actually did you a favour? 3. How can you learn to use your intuition to know if people are levelling with you?

Inspiration

Inspiration can truly come in a myriad of forms, spanning the vast expanse of human experience and beyond. Often, people yearn for grand revelations, hoping for a booming voice from the Heavens above, accompanied by thunder and lightning, to guide them on their journey through life. While such displays of inspiration might seem awe-inspiring, they are not the only channels through which profound inspiration can flow!

In fact, inspiration, like a gentle breeze, can whisper softly, barely noticeable at first, but capable of carrying the most profound messages. A child's innocent poem can tug at the heartstrings and ignite the flames of creativity within us. The lyrics of a song, weaving emotions and stories into harmonious melodies, can move us to tears or lift our spirits to soaring heights. A single piece of music can paint the canvas of our minds with colours of imagination and evoke memories of bygone days.

The search for inspiration can be a lifelong pursuit, akin to an endless treasure hunt, and the Universe itself stands as a tireless teacher, always seeking to impart its wisdom upon us. Yet, the onus lies upon us to open our eyes and hearts, to keenly observe the world around us, and to recognise the subtle whispers of inspiration that weave through the fabric of existence. It is through this process of attentive observation that we become attuned to the lessons that life is constantly offering.

One night, a few days before I was due to give an important speech, the Universe bestowed upon me a special gift. As a Councillor, I was due to deliver a speech that would illuminate the impact of losing someone to the harrowing illness of HIV/AIDS. In the depths of the night, around 4 a.m., I was wide awake, and the speech appeared in my mind, fully formed, as if it had been whispered to me.

Compelled by the need to write down the speech I had received, I got up and I committed those profound words to paper. The speech recounted the poignant tale of my dear friend, Peter, a man of loving generosity and remarkable character, who succumbed to an AIDS-related illness in the prime of his life, in his 30s. Peter's kindness had touched my life in ways words could scarcely describe, and his influence had transformed my life, leading me to the love of my life - my husband. It was a story that I wanted to share, a tribute to a life lived so magnificently, but cut tragically short.

When the day arrived to address the gathering of Brighton and Hove City Council, I rose to speak with Peter's story in my mind and on the paper in front of met. As I spoke, the room fell into a hushed silence, as if the very air held its breath to listen. My intention wasn't to create dramatic effect; it was merely to share a tale that had touched me deeply.

Yet, to my astonishment, the impact was palpable, like ripples spreading across a tranquil pond. My words resonated with the souls of those present, evoking empathy, stirring emotions, and inspiring action. It was a testament to the power of genuine inspiration, a force that transcends the boundaries of time and space, connecting us all in a shared tapestry of humanity.

That earlier night, when inspiration coursed through me, was not an isolated incident. It was a reminder that inspiration is a wondrous wellspring that knows no bounds. When we are open to its presence, it finds us in unexpected moments, guiding our pens, voices, and hearts.

Let us then embrace the gentle breeze, the child's poem, the song's lyrics, and the harmonies of music, for they are the conduits of inspiration that carry us forward on this magnificent journey called life. With vigilant eyes and receptive hearts, let's seek inspiration's ever-present embrace and let it spark the flames of creativity and change within us. For in this dance with inspiration, we become not just recipients of wisdom but also its benevolent messengers, passing on the torch of inspiration to others, lifting their souls, and brightening the path of their journey as well.

Questions to ponder

1.  How can you receive guidance that always points you in the right direction?

2.  How can you find the inspiration you are looking for?

3.  When have you trusted your intuition and it has paid off for you?

Freedom from Fear

Fear, a potent force that looms over the human experience, can be the biggest obstacle standing between us and the boundless joy that the fruits of Spirit can bestow. The Universe, in its eternal wisdom, orchestrates the symphony of life, guiding us towards the paths that are aligned with our highest good. However, fear erects a formidable barrier, hindering the manifestation of many blessings.

Fear manifests in various forms, each capable of imposing self-inflicted limits and thwarting the fulfilment of our deepest aspirations. The fear of failure, with its cold grip on our hearts, discourages us from taking risks and exploring uncharted territories. Lack of confidence, like a relentless shadow, shrouds our potential and hinders us from realising our true worth. The fear of the transition after death clouds our minds with uncertainty, obscuring the eternal truths that Spirit seeks to share with us.

Yet, the key to unlocking the treasures of our birthright lies in the act of banishing fear from our lives. Undeniably, it is no easy feat, for fear has a way of entwining itself with our very essence. Nevertheless, through unwavering determination and a resolute spirit, we can free ourselves from the shackles of fear, allowing Spirit to usher in the blessings that await us.

Spirit gently imparts timeless wisdom upon us, emphasising the significance of trust and faith in constructing a life of enduring substance. As we attentively observe the world around us, we begin to witness the tangible results that justify our belief in the guiding force of Spirit. Remarkably, we realise that even the seemingly insurmountable challenges can be overcome when we embrace faith as our steadfast companion.

Consider, for instance, the prevailing belief among many that they cannot muster the strength to lift a heavy car or relinquish a deeply ingrained and challenging habit. Yet, when faced with the dire situation of a loved one trapped beneath a vehicle, a seemingly superhuman strength emerges, driven by the potent force of love and urgency. Similarly, confronting the harsh reality of illness can prompt profound transformations, motivating individuals to abandon self-destructive behaviours like smoking, paving the way for renewed health and vitality.

It is a fallacy to think that we must await extreme circumstances to spur us into making life-altering changes. In truth, the power to transform lies within us, ready to be harnessed at any moment. The path to a better quality of life is paved with proactive choices and the willingness to embrace change sooner rather than later.

A pivotal moment in this journey of conquering fear occurred in the year 1992 when I stumbled upon a discounted book titled 'Feel the Fear and Do it Anyway' by Susan Jeffers, during a visit to New York City. Initially, I left the book untouched for about two years. One day, looking for something to read, when I finally turned its pages, it was a revelation. The book dismantled the facade of fear, revealing it not as an unconquerable beast, but as an ephemeral construct that could be dissected, examined, and ultimately vanquished.

The pursuit of fearlessness is often portrayed as a simple feat — a matter of "facing our fears." Yet, as any courageous soul can attest, the journey is far from straightforward. For me, the path to overcoming the fear of public speaking and delivering spiritual messages in public was paved with one simple truth: repetition. It was through relentless practice, through doing it over and over again, that the shackles of fear began to crumble.

Still, as human nature dictates, the shadows of doubt and insecurity often loom, casting doubt on our abilities and self-worth. In such moments, I return to the central tenet of 'Feel the Fear and Do It Anyway,' which serves as a guiding Light. It reminds me that life, with its twists and turns, may present challenges beyond our wildest imaginings. However, armed with the profound understanding that I have the strength and resilience to handle whatever life hands me, I march forward with determination.

In the end, fear may be an ever-present companion, but we have the power to alter its influence on our lives. By embracing faith, trust, and perseverance, we allow the fruits of Spirit to bloom in our hearts, and the joy that was once obscured by fear will become an enduring source of strength and inspiration, guiding us towards a life of fulfilment and purpose.


Questions to ponder

1.    When have you overcome your fear and been able to move forward?

2.    What is your worst fear?

3.    Who are you afraid of and why?

## Meditation

Meditation, a sacred ritual that allows us to transcend the noise of the outer world, beckons us to embrace the whispers of our inner selves. However, the art of meditation is not without its challenges, and many individuals find themselves disheartened by the seemingly insurmountable task of stilling their minds. Yet, meditation is a profound practice that unfolds over time, beckoning us to delve deeper into the realm of the Spirit.

The Spirit World, with its benevolent inhabitants, stands ready to draw close to us during our moments of meditation. They seek to bestow upon us the gifts of joy, peace, and guidance. However, like any skill, meditation requires cultivation and patience. It is not a hurried sprint but a gentle, persistent journey of self-discovery and communion with the divine.

One need not approach meditation as a daunting, time-consuming task. On the contrary, it can be as simple as taking a few moments each day to sit quietly, allowing the mind to settle like a calm pond reflecting the sky above. Quieting the mind is a skill that blossoms with practice, and as we make space for this contemplative endeavour regularly, insights from begin to unfurl like blooming flowers.

Yet, in the pursuit of stillness, many individuals find themselves burdened by self-criticism, fearing they might not be doing it "right." The truth is that meditation is not a rigid formula with a definitive right or wrong. Rather, it is a receptive state where we allow ourselves to receive from Spirit that which we truly need. Every meditation session is unique, and the messages, feelings, and experiences that come forth are tailor-made for our soul's growth and well-being.

At times, the mind may wander, like a curious child exploring the vast landscape of thoughts. When this happens, there is no cause for dismay or self-judgment. Instead, we gently acknowledge the wandering mind, tenderly bringing it back to the stillness and focus that meditation entails. The wandering mind is a natural part of the human experience, and there is no shame in its presence. The only misstep lies in allowing the wandering thoughts to embrace us completely, veering us off the path of meditation.

For those who feel as though they have not "received" anything during their meditation, it is essential to reconsider what receiving truly entails. Perhaps, in those sacred moments of meditation, Spirit gifted them with ten minutes of tranquility and peace - a precious commodity in a world often dominated by chaos. The absence of a grand revelation does not signify failure. The gift of peace is in itself a profound blessing, nurturing the soul and recharging the spirit.

Indeed, meditation is a journey of self-awareness and spiritual awakening, and like any journey, it requires patience, resilience, and an open heart. As we venture into the realms of inner seeing, feeling, and expressing, we open ourselves to a deeper understanding of our essence and our connection to the Universe. Meditation, when practiced with sincerity and consistency, reveals the richness and beauty of our inner world, mirroring the boundless wonders of the cosmos.

So, let us embrace meditation, not as an arduous task, but as a soul-nourishing communion with the Universe. Through each moment of stillness, we grow closer to the loving embrace of the Spirit World and discover the profound wisdom that resides within us. And as we continue to meditate, we will witness the blossoming of our souls, adorned with the petals of peace, joy, and guidance that have been lovingly bestowed upon us by the ever-present spirits and the boundless expanse of the cosmos.

Questions to ponder

1.    If you knew celebrities like Oprah, Paul McCartney and Orlando Bloom meditated, how would that knowledge help you make it part of your own daily life?

2. What would the ability to access simple wisdom mean to you and your life?

3. How could you help yourself and others if you received guidance on the questions you face?

Gratitude

Gratitude, like a key to the Universe's treasure trove, unlocks the door to boundless possibilities. It is the art of appreciating and acknowledging the blessings that currently grace our lives, paving the way for even greater gifts to arrive in our journey. Gratitude is not about turning a blind eye to the challenges we face or pretending that everything is perfect. Rather, it is a conscious choice to recognise and value the abundance, no matter how small, that enriches our lives in the present moment.

Life is a tapestry woven with various threads of experiences, and it is not uncommon to find imperfections in the fabric of our existence. We may reside in a home that falls short of our dreams or yearn for financial prosperity beyond our current means. Nevertheless, gratitude beckons us to pause and appreciate the roof over our heads, no matter how humble, and the money that sustains us, no matter how limited. By embracing gratitude for what we have now, we create a fertile ground for the seeds of abundance to take root and flourish.

 The practice of gratitude need not be confined to occasional moments of reflection. Rather, it is a powerful spiritual tool that can be woven into the fabric of our daily lives. Cultivating an attitude of gratitude throughout the day, like a fragrant garden, blossoms with opportunities and miracles. One beautiful way to embrace gratitude is to compile a list of things for which we are thankful. In doing so, we paint a vibrant canvas of appreciation, honouring the intricate details of our existence.

By undertaking this spiritual practice consistently for 30 days, we initiate a profound alchemy within ourselves and the world around us. Gratitude acts as a catalyst, catalysing important changes that ripple through our lives, transforming the mundane into the extraordinary. As we express gratitude for our current circumstances, the Universe takes notice and aligns itself with our desires, conspiring to bring us closer to our ideals and aspirations.

In the realm of the metaphysical, gratitude holds a mystical power that attracts synchronicities, fortuitous encounters, and serendipitous events. It is as if the cosmos responds to our gratitude with a resounding "yes," offering a dance of co-creation that surpasses the boundaries of the known. As we bask in the glow of gratitude, the Universe responds in kind, showering us with even more reasons to be grateful.

Moreover, the practice of gratitude radiates beyond our individual lives, touching the hearts and souls of those around us. Our expression of thankfulness becomes an invisible thread, weaving through the tapestry of humanity, uniting us in a profound connection of shared appreciation. As we offer gratitude to others, they, too, are inspired to embrace their blessings, creating a beautiful tapestry of interconnectedness and compassion.

Ultimately, gratitude is a gateway to self-awareness and spiritual growth. Through its transformative power, we shed the cloak of discontent and embrace the innate beauty of our existence. The simple act of giving thanks magnifies the blessings we possess, propelling us towards the manifestation of our dreams. Gratitude is the torch that illuminates our path, guiding us through the labyrinth of life with a heart full of wonder and appreciation.

So, let us embark on this sacred journey of gratitude, embracing each moment as an opportunity to give thanks and receive with an open heart. In doing so, we embrace the essence of life itself, like a radiant sun casting its warm glow on all that surrounds us. With every breath, with every gesture of thankfulness, we welcome the Universe's bounty into our lives, and we stand as co-creators of a world filled with love, abundance, and infinite possibilities.

Questions to ponder

1. List 10 things for which you are currently grateful

2. What things have happened and are happening in your life right now that you cannot imagine ever feeling grateful for?

3. With hindsight we can often see the benefit that came from a difficult situation. When has that happened to you?

## Prayer

Prayer, a sacred connection that transcends the boundaries of the material realm, offers us a profound communion with the Spirit. Through prayer, we open the channels of our hearts, allowing the divine presence to draw close and envelop us in its loving embrace. Whether we seek to offer gratitude for the blessings bestowed upon us, request guidance in times of uncertainty, or ask for something specific to enhance our lives, prayer becomes a sanctuary where our soul finds solace and our spirit finds strength.

The act of praying on a regular basis is akin to tending to a Divine garden within us. Like a gardener nurturing the seeds of faith and hope, we cultivate a fertile ground for spiritual growth. In this sacred space, we can sow the seeds of our desires, knowing that they will bloom and blossom at the perfect time, guided by the hand of the loving Spirit. Through prayer, we become co-creators of our destiny, aligning ourselves with the ever-present cosmic forces that dance in harmony with our intentions.

Moreover, the power of prayer extends beyond our personal lives, reaching out like a gentle ripple in the ocean of humanity. Sending absent healing to those near and far is a beautiful opportunity to serve and bestow love upon those who may be feeling bereft or lonely. As we open our hearts and extend our intentions of healing and compassion, the collective consciousness of mankind experiences a profound shift towards harmony and unity.

The act of healing transcends the barriers of distance and touches the souls of countless individuals, radiating love and light throughout the world.

Amidst the pursuit of accomplishment and achievement, it is vital to remain mindful of the tapestry of life that weaves around us. The world is not merely a stage for our achievements; it is a canvas where we co-create moments of joy, passion, and connection. In the realm of work, it is not solely about carrying out tasks, but about fostering meaningful relationships and embracing endeavors that fill us with enthusiasm and purpose. When we raise a child, it is not merely about nurturing a future adult; it is about reveling in the boundless love and wonder that an infant brings into our lives.

By embracing these moments of connection and joy, we awaken to the innate richness of life. Every experience becomes an opportunity to engage with the world in a way that transcends the mundane and touches the sacred. We become fully present, savouring each precious instant, and through this mindful presence, we discover the profound beauty hidden within the tapestry of everyday life.

In this grand tapestry of existence, each thread of experience is woven intricately, forming an intricate mosaic of growth, love, and spiritual awakening. We are both creators and witnesses to the unfolding masterpiece of life, and every step we take, every prayer we utter, and every act of love we share contributes to the grandeur of this cosmic masterpiece.

So, let us continue to embrace prayer as a sacred bridge between our souls and the divine. Through prayer, we traverse the realms of the seen and unseen, basking in the warmth of spiritual communion. Let us extend our love and healing intentions beyond ourselves, becoming vessels of divine grace and comfort for those who yearn for solace. And as we journey through life's triumphs and challenges, let us remain ever-mindful of the sacred moments that surround us, for in these moments, we encounter the essence of the divine, and we become active participants in the dance of creation itself.

Questions to ponder

1. What benefit do you believe could you gain from being in constant touch with Spirit?

2. What would a simple prayer of thanks sound like to you?

3. What would you like to talk (pray) to Spirit about?

## Conclusion

I hope this eBook has been helpful to you.

Email me to let me know how this book helped you and to let me know your story. It is time to lift your burden!

With Love, light and blessings

Brian Oxley

Printed in Great Britain
by Amazon